The Book of Nna: III

© Kofi Piesie Research Team. © Same Tree Different Branch

Kofi Piesie/Mossi Warrior Clan

Copyright 2020 by Kofi Piesie Research Team

All right reserved. No Part of this book may be reproduced or transmitted in any form or by any means, electronic or mechanical, including photocopying, recordings, or by any information storage and retrieval systems without the written permission of the publisher.

Printed in the United States of America

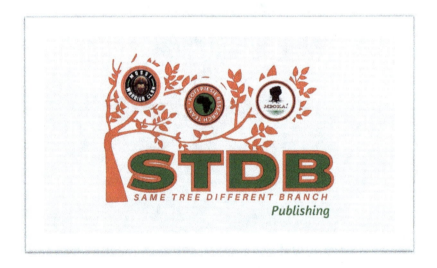

Table of Contents

CHAPTER I: Reflections on the Masculine Energy and the Fundamentals of Resistance......................7

CHAPTER II: How the lack of access to Information technology (IT) is Destroying Traditional AfRaKa..20

CHAPTER I11: Merging IT and Education for the complete Liberation of AfRaKa..........................31

CHAPTER IV: The Importance of AfRaKaN Investment and the need for Retribution/Reparations.42

CHAPTER V: Why foreign states should transfer Knowledge, Technology and back to AfRaKa.........55

CHAPTER VI: The need in AfRAKA for more Technology and Research Centers.......................64

CHAPTER VII: Using Information Technology to combat the hegemony in international trade relations..71

CHAPTER VIII: Is antagonism the primary catalyst behind the AfRaKaN Information Age?......................78

CHAPTER IX: Solar Powered and Efficient Transportation in the battle against Climate Change...84

CHAPTER X: A Brief Look at AfRaKaN Initiatives to Explore Space..93

CHAPTER XI: CONCLUSION.......................101

DEDICATION

In the honor of Iya this book is dedicated to Nna, my arakunrin Chris, my omo Tedros, the great Atsuko Makane Faye as well as my immediate ebi (Isaiah, Saba, Rahel and iyawo Zebib) and extended awon ebi like bro Garfield Reid, Ankh West, Kofi Piesie, Ini-Herit Shawn Khalfani and the Mossi Warrior Clan, the Daggar Squad, Pseudo Killas, Science with Shawn, SaRa Suten Seti, Young Nisut Sheena Lynne, Kecia Jones, Thurston Hargrove, John Pitts and all my supporters on social media as well as all of those who seek truth, wisdom and understanding and to whom I owe the greatest debt.......... I would also like to thank the medical and emergency teams as well as the staff from Lawrenceville Emergencies, Gwinnett Medical Center Glancy, Rehab Center and Northside Hospital here in the Greater Metropolitan area........I ask you to remember that.........Tomorrow........is not a given........but yesterday was.......and today.....is being given...........

Those AfRaKaNs who walked the plank

Oh, how I remember that day
When those AfRaKaNs walked the plank
Oh, how I remember Goree
When those AfRaKaNs walked the plank

So many drowned in the Great Ocean
Are those AfRaKaNs who walked the plank
So many kept their devotion
Are those AfRaKaNs who walked the plank

Now many live in the States
as those AfRaKaNs who walked the plank
Must never make the mistake and forget
Those AfRaKaNs who walked the plank

CHAPTER I

CHAPTER I: Reflections on the Masculine Energy and the Fundamentals of Resistance

At the end of publishing The Book of Nna: Vol. II, I discovered some troubling but liberating news. For most of my existence, I had been told that a eniyan by the name of Jack was my Nna.

After taking a DNA test, however, I discovered that Jack had actually told me the truth and that oun was not my nna. Still, maybe out of sympathy and a sense of inherited AfRaKaN values, Jack continued to maintain a connection with me even through extended ebi ties, even though it was a distant connection. This was a direct and clear example of how inherited traditional AfRaKaN culture and values resonate within most AfRaKaNs in America, whether they are conscious of it or not.

At the same, while I was unaware of my DNA heritage for most of my existence, I maintained an AfRaCentric perspective in terms of my identity and values thanks to my ebi and the teachings of the great Atsuko/Hem Neter Dr., who introduced me to Kemetic studies as part of my educational experience in general while I was attending Central State University.

In fact, my concept of existence, i.e., my understanding of "being," was defined and driven by the positive and negative aspects of my experiences with Dr. Lewis, Jack, and my ebi in general. Something that stood out to me, which I realized much later, was just how significant the development of my skills and knowledge, including my knowledge of Jack, had shaped my consciousness. Jack had experienced AfRaKa and had been stationed at a U.S. Navy base known as Kanyo Station in Eritrea. Kanyo Station was a part of the US government's strategy to protect the colonialist control of the flow of water routes coming thru the Suez Canal and the flow of gold and oil, which was being abstracted from what is now referred to as "Ethiopia" and is also a direct byproduct of the Cauc-asian perspective that has been imposed on "East" or the traditional AfRaKaN " Nubia.

My studies as an undergrad motivated me to be more interested in AfRaKaN Etan, which also lead me to be particularly interested in Ethiopia, which I had assumed was TaNehesi, Nubia, and Cush. Furthermore, I also developed a strong interest in AfRaKaN culture and languages and the etan of AfRaKa in general.

To this extent, my perspective and scholarship were heavily impacted by the knowledge presented to me by the great Hem Neter Dr. Joseph E. Lewis. Under this atsuko's direction I began to study as much as I could in regard to AfRaKaN history. Atsuko Lewis and other awon atsuko at CSU encouraged my to develop my understanding of AfRaKa. I should mention here that Dr. Lee Ingham and Dr. Jeff Crawford exposed me to the foundation of philosophical methods and analysis, i.e., the principles of reasoning, logic, and the fundamentals of methodology. This allowed me to become well-prepared and critical in terms of my studies of etan. I concentrated my studies on liberation theology by studying the greats awon Atsuko, like Dr. Ben, John Henry Clarke, Cheikh Anta Diop, Walter Williams, and liberation theologists like Paulo Freire and Frantz Fanon. These scholars clearly understood the impact of religion on AfRaKa and were able to function within the constraints to develop the founding principles of a truly AfRaKaN methodology, i.e., perspective with regards to addressing the global machine of imperialism.

In addition, I should also add other great Hem Neteru such as J.A. Rogers, George G.M. James, and John G. Jackson.

However, it was when I met Molefi Asante and was introduced to the Afracentric Idea that I began to focus heavily on methodology, which I see as the natural growth of AfRaKaN consciousness and as well as my own intellectual development.

The more I studied, the more I realized that AfRacentricity had always been an essential component of my consciousness and has made number of valuable contributions in terms of maturation and the development of my own sense of an AfRaKan. As a result, I continued my studies with the goal of being able to return to AfRaKa permanently.

My studies of philosophy and methodology allowed me to understand the importance of conceptualizing a completely independent (AfRaKaN) perspective. This is a perspective that no individual can claim ownership of as it is an essential component of the AfRaKan concept of existence that became dormant due to the imposition of colonialism.

While in Grad School and teaching at various locations, I came to the conclusion that this approach to scholarship would have to be free from Eurasiancentrism and its poison. I realized that AfRaKa needed to abstract itself from the shackles of Imperialism to achieve this goal. Thus there is an AfRaKaN approach that would have to extend from traditional AfRaKaN contributions to history and an overall perspective that would include both knowledge and science.

During this time, I also concluded that colonialism had introduced existence to what has been referred to as Existential Imperialism in my earlier books. I must also mention that this led me to a unique understanding and appreciation of just how vital Information Technology (IT) was/is in restoring a traditional AfRaKaN perspective of existence.

In this regard, not only does technological development have the potential to lead AfRaKa towards a path of liberation, but also provides a good foundation for preserving traditional AFraKan perspectives regarding existence. What we could then conclude would serve as the primary building block to the AfRaKaN Identity must be fueled by its own traditional perspective.

It is important to remember that we must incorporate modernized values, mores, etc....into our methodology.

I must acknowledge that since opening my mouth after leaving the hospital and therapy, I have experienced a very difficult situation. In fact, after returning to my ebi, I have been treated like "shit" or like a felon by this system which is unfortunate because the interest and goal of educating eniyan about climate change is critical when it comes to preventing an existential level event.

Regardless of the obstacles, I am still committed to the goal of promoting awareness of global warming. This motivation has me convinced that IT and science, in general, offers the best possible option for existence to escape the paradigms of intellectual imperialism. These obstacles leave our collective consciousness trapped in shackles of indoctrination that lead to impoverishment, crime and sexual deviance, and an overall decay of modern society.

The objective of this book is to emphasize the value of identity (culture) preservation by adapting technology and a new pedagogy within educational sectors. We will also present the development of my IT skills and how they shaped my concept of TaNeheSi by incorporating Yoruba principles in my method just like I did in The Book of Iya (Vol.1,2,3) as well as Vol.1 of The Book of Nna.

Again, the purpose here has always been the preservation of Traditional AfRaKaN cultural perspective, i.e., a perspective that incorporates indigenous languages, customs, mores of AfRaKa cultures and civilizations. This must include an evaluation of ancient Ta-Merry, Ta-Seti, Ta-Nehesi, DMT, Nubia, and Cushite perspectives. We must understand the responsibility we have as scholars to be blatantly honest and accurate in terms of our perspectives and methodology. The outcome will be the fostering of tools that will assist in the resurgence, restoration and preservation of traditional AfRaKaN culture which by no means is an easy task. It does, however, offer hope and positive outcomes for many, especially among AfRaKa and non-AfRaKaN from an existential perspective. I fear that many have not had the opportunity in the Americas to read my texts and may not understand the perspective presented as it contradicts the mainstream Eurasian paradigm, which again, is homosexual indeed..........just like the Heka Kasu.

Nevertheless, we must continue to move forward due to the need of addressing the threat of climate change and its potential to severely impact existence as we know it. It should also be noted that this is not about any form of religion or any chosen "death-" or "life-" styles but is based on the reality that religion itself is unscientific and has created a vacuum in our consciousness has been usurped by imperialism which results in a lack or dismissal of scientific principles and methodology.

This is a by-product of CaucAsian imperialism and must be addressed if we are to be serious about the liberation of all things AfRaKaN. Consequently, a critique of the AfRaKaN addiction to religion shows that we have become entirely dependent on and subdued by myth and religious themes that are complete nonsense and contradicts the fundamental principles of the scientific methodology, i.e., observation and experimentation as well as the laws of Netcher (nature).

Religion supports belief, whereas science firmly supports observation and experimentation which sits at the foundation of the scientific methodology and knowledge with conclusions that can be verified or falsified.

As an IT Specialist, for most of my existence, I was never a faithful follower of religion and obtained a very scientific orientation thru my education and experience including living on our ebi's farm-life, There, mathematics, Science, Physics, Math, Logic and Philosophy, in general, were essential element components of farm life. This led to the formation of rebellion that was incorporated into the AfRaKan Identity and allowed the carving out of an AFRAKaN perspective within the context of the American (HK) experience. I am sure this is the case with other oppressed eniyan in the Americas. Of course the one who controls the pen also controls the narrative, so it's essential to investigate for yourself.

Instead, far too many of us will not study and may not realize it due to the lack of education. Still, our consciousness has been colonized and subdued by the various forms of pseudo-science and illogical beliefs as opposed to traditional knowledge and cultural systems. The AfRaKaN in America identity has been usurped into the Germanic scheme of "Blackness." You will not find "Black" in AfRaKaN language. So, when the AfRaKaN refers to her/his existence as "black" not only are we colonizing ourselves but opening the door for the colonization of AfRaKa.

There is an attempt to erase the concept of traditional living and existential uniqueness from reality as a whole. One of the dangers of technology, especially the media, is that it can produce a monopoly driven by a monolithic perspective of existence.

 If you review traditional AfRaKaN cultural systems, you will see that they are very scientific in nature, and AfRaKa is a pluralistic continue. A key element of AfRaCentific thought/culture is that it allows diversity and pluralism. This is especially true before the invasion by the various clans of the "HK."   I am convinced that this conclusion is true for most eniyan and is important and true for most of the other cultures of Geb including those who may not be AfRaKaN in general. We should allow space for others to speak for themselves and encourage multicultural exchange.

My goal here is not to produce a replica of Eurasian imperialism but to create opportunities for other traditions and cultures to develop and articulate their own perspectives using their own methodologies.

This will allow us to stand firmly and at least be unified in scientific terms. To accomplish this, we will discuss the potential that IT and technology have in general to offer to existence from an AfRaKaN perspective. AfRaKa needs Technology, and while IT provides much promise for AfRAKa, it can only do so if AfRaKaNs take the initiative to escape indoctrination and its colonial origins and pursue knowledge-based initiatives. This also suggests that AfRaKa must not become an imperialist continent but stand firm to defend her traditional pre-colonial identity.

In this regard, the AfRaKaN identity has been attacked, and technology, especially IT offers the chance to confront the threat head-on. I ask that you reserve judgment regarding the quality or value of this book until you have read all the books in The Book of Iya series, Vol.1 of the Book of Nna series, and the other books, including those by my brilliant publishers.

And remember, whether we like it or not, this is shaped and driven by technological interpretation of AfRaKa's development needs to demonstrate what is required to extract ourselves from a system of global imperialism that affects much of Geb's population. So, I will demonstrate the promise that technology has in this regard and how we have reached a great moment in Pr Ankh to introduce an AfRaKaN age of renewal in which science and technology are returned to balance.

CHAPTER II

CHAPTER II: How the lack of access to Information technology (IT) is Destroying Traditional AfRaKa

Recent studies indicate that only 1/3 of Afraka has access to the Internet and other forms of digital technology. Not only does the lack of access impede the technological growth of nations, but it also limits the ability of AfRaKaNs to promote and preserve their own socio-cultural concepts of identity, i.e., their traditional and cultural expressions of existence. An excellent example of this is how the majority of apps are being developed in

English, French, German, Spanish, Chinese, and Korean, and you find many languages tools in such languages but very few in traditional AfRaKaN languages such as Yoruba, Akan, Wolof, Xhosa, Bambara or other Bantu forms of expression.

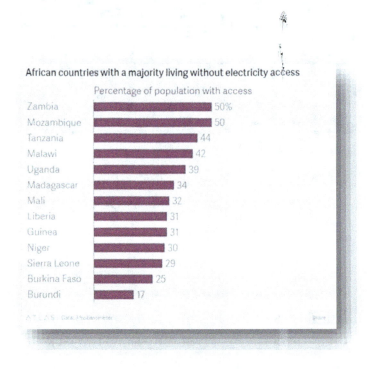

African countries with a majority living without electricity access

Percentage of population with access

Country	
Zambia	50%
Mozambique	50
Tanzania	44
Malawi	42
Uganda	39
Madagascar	34
Mali	32
Liberia	31
Guinea	31
Niger	30
Sierra Leone	29
Burkina Faso	25
Burundi	17

There are many in the AfRaKaN Geb (excuse me………I meant AfRaKaN Worlid) that concede to the false notion that Hebrew, Arab and other Caucasian languages are parts of traditional AfRaKaN culture and reflect concepts of existence that are AfRaKaN. "Man" and "Wombed Man," as well as "color" consciousness, is, a perfect example of this. Colonial powers have stripped the AfRaKaN from the power to define reality in AfRaKaN terms. This includes the present definition of the AfRaKa and how it's been demarcated. ("Worlid") is a perfect example of this failure to view AfRaKA from its own cultural perspective.

This results in the complete usurping of the AfRAKaN "being" by an Anglophone or Cauc-Asian linguistic expression of "being," resulting in self-imposed imperialism. In addition, we must consider that WEB and Application Development, as well as social media platforms like Youtube, Facebook, and others, are almost entirely Eurasian-centered and biased in an imperialist perspective.

When we concede to Caucasian tools of expression, we are also conceding to caucasian hegemony of consciousness and its domination and control over much of the epistemology of existence or being as we know it.

Religion and ignorance have left us in a state of vulnerability when it comes to technological development. For example, how much technology is AfRaKa producing compared to what it consumes, i.e., imports?

Another excellent example of the hegemony in this technological vacuum is the AfRaKaN dependency on Eurasian concepts of being where instead of utilizing AfRaKaN points of reference, referring to ourselves from AfRaKaN perspectives like Yoruba, Akan, Wolofi...etc. AfRaKaNs abroad and at home concede to referring to themselves as "black" or brown. And Eurasian victims of the same tool imposed on states that are dominated by an elite group (caucasian imperialist) will refer to themselves as "white" or "yellow." This denies the victims of imperialism their innate right and power of existence to define themselves according to their own cultural heritage. However, IT allows us to escape this and restore the power of self-definition that traditional societies once had before being colonized.

My studies at Howard and employment at various universities and international development agencies like the UNECA provided me with opportunities to evaluate a number of development issues, such as debt and how those nations that sponsor these loans are able to hold these clients hostage and use debt as leverage as a means to gain access to AfRaKaN resources. Borrowing is equivalent to a flag of surrender that puts the borrower in a weak position that compromises the recipient state's development agenda.

In this regard, experience at international organizations and initiatives allowed me opportunities to witness the potential imperialist/donor states to manipulate and control colonized eniyan. From an AfRaKaN perspective, this suggests that one of the more effective ways of reversing the damage caused by imperialism is the supporting AfRaKaN initiatives that are filled with Information Technology and driven by traditional culture. Where unscientific paradisms have left us in a stagmated existence, Technology can be used to offer the digitization of infrastructure and address issues associated with brain drain, depopulation, as well as communication and trade. For example, converting the libraries of Timbuktu and Ancient Kemet into other traditional AfRaKaN languages would allow us to digitize the data and then develop Apps that preserve such content for longevity. Returning to tradition will empower AfRaKa to become a standaed and modern for development in a new Information driven society.

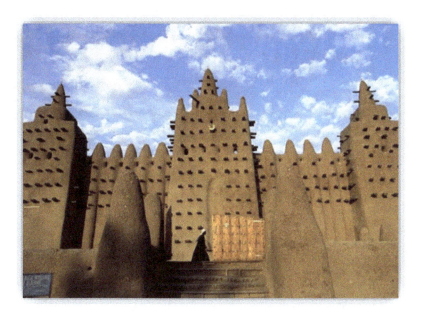

This alone would expand AfRaKaN intellectualism beyond the confines of the shackles and scares imposed on the continent by imperialism and the colonizer's religion. Again, religion is an agent of imperialism.

Based on a review of the chart shown below, it becomes clear that AfRaKa is far behind in terms of technological development

The World's Most Innovative Countries

2021 ranking of the Global Innovation Index
(100 = most innovative)

Country	Score
Switzerland	65.5
Sweden	63.1
U.S.	61.3
UK	59.8
South Korea	59.3
Netherlands	58.6
Finland	58.4
Singapore	57.8

Takes into account human capital, institutions, technology and creative output,
market and business sophistication, among others
Source: World Intellectual Property Organization

Since the beginning of the colonial experience, the lack of Technology has produced a situation where:

"As of summer 2021, 149 World Bank projects are active in 34 African countries to support the emergence of a vibrant, inclusive and safe digital economy. The projects are diverse and robust and help to narrow the digital divide through electronic identification and banking, mobile money services, family support, training, and mentoring through digital hubs and universities."

This is important because, in the absence of a new Information driven paradigm, access to the information needed to lift AfRaKa and other oppressed eniyan will remain hampered by financial and intellectual poverty. For example

"Too many Africans cannot access the technology they need for school, work, health, or financial services. The pandemic has underscored the vulnerability of the digitally excluded, who have a more challenging time accessing vital information, including health education and e-commerce.

A 2020 World Bank and GSMA study demonstrated the positive impact of mobile broadband on welfare and poverty reduction in Africa, using data from Nigeria, the largest mobile market on the continent. The percentage of households below the extreme poverty line drops by about 4 percentage points after one year of mobile broadband coverage, and about 7 percentage points after two or more years, in large part due to increased participation in the labor force during that time. Broadband infrastructure is a key driver of jobs and productivity, especially in rural and remote areas."(2)

The vital thing to note here is that technology can be an essential aspect of AfRaKa's revitalization as defined by AfRaKaNs. AfRaKa must develop the knowledge of producing their own technology to address development needs without being dependent and enslaved by imports.

Currently, what we see exactly is that a few businesses from the Colonizer's camp are using financial systems in favor of a select minority while the majority of eniyan around Geb are subjected to subservient states of existence.

In this regard, it is essential that IT be utilized to re-establish traditional and independent financial systems. This would allow AfRaKa to liberate itself from the global imposition of existential imperialism.

CHAPTER III

CHAPTER III: Merging IT and Education for the complete Liberation of AfRaKa

Much of the struggle regarding the decolonization of AfRaKa has been focused on building up wealth. However, while obtaining wealth and financial independence is important and needs to be accomplished as an aspect of AfRaKaN development, the acquisition of wealth can also be problematic as it has the potential to lead many towards greed, nepotism, dictatorship, tyranny, and other forms of exploitation, i.e., moral decay.

This allows the class of select individuals that was mentioned earlier to become wealthy elitists who can be either foreign or local. For quite some time now, the existence for AfRaKa as well as that of many impoverished nations, has been plagued by an international system of exploitation where a minority has benefitted from an allegiance to their imperialist masters who, again, can be both foreign and local.

Many AfRaKaN "thinkers" like Kwame Nkruma along with others like George Padmore, Marcus Garvey, and Leopold Senghor were, in fact, inspired not only by the philosophical teachings of the abolishment moment in the US but were also influenced by the call for liberation by a global resistance movement. In other words, the collective energy that produced the call for abolition and decolonization is now demanding reform and repatriation to address existential imperialism, i.e., poverty and the erasing of traditional culture and values.

In response, the imperialists continue to use covert, secretive, and immoral measures to infiltrate various groups who advocate for AfRaKaN liberation both here in the US as a reflection of traditional AfRaKaN values. This can also be applied to the call for justice made by poor Asian and European states.

 Patrice La-Mumba, Amilcal Cabral, and Steve Biko were all assassinated, while others have been reduced to absolute impoverishment, like Marcus Garvey. This results from both existential imperialism and the policies of control instituted by the ruling elitists.

It should be noted that the benefactors and primary designers who control this global system are representatives of a financial paradigm that represents and promotes American and Brit-ish interests with the ultimate goal of global domination.

From an AfRaKaN perspective, this provides credence to the perspective that for AfRaKa, education has the potential to serve as a remedy that can and should be used to address dependency issues and financial and intellectual domination based on a perspective of European intellectualism. Their noted Philosophers like John Locke, Adam Smith, Max Weber, Karl Marx, and Joseph Stalin were all poisoned by their addiction to Eurocentrism and maybe because it is derived from the Caucasian perspective and sits at the foundation of their identity.

This is why a collective expression of resistance has the potential to serve as the most significant opportunity to project and promote a better stance of resistance for oppressed populations in their interests against indoctrination.

However, this will not be easy due to the penetration of foreign ideas, institutions, and perspectives into the continent. The agents of imperialism continue to be anti-AfRaKan by nature. They are driven by a desire to extract as much resources and wealth from   AfRaKaN and Asian populations as possible. Again, it's crucial for the poor in other groupings to conduct their own research and join other progressive movements by speaking up for themselves without fearing reprisal.

Furthermore, because these locals are perceived to be either savage or beasts that are incapable of critical thinking and have never made any contribution to collective intellectualism or contributing anything to civilization as well, it becomes convenient and easy to then justify that such (AfRaKaN) individuals are disposable and can be treated as subservient.

Technology, however, can be a great tool that supports the liberation of AfRaKa from the ignorance and poverty imposed by Asiatic imperialism.

In fact, not fiction, AfRaKan has the potential, just like any other eniyan, to produce oun's own technology similar to what our Asian "friends" have been able to accomplish ever since World War II. We must liberate ourselves from the stigmas of subjugation that suggests that science and technology are in contrast with Netcher.

This is why the ability to demand reparations for both our enslavement and colonialism is very important, as funding is essential to financial stability and establishing IT-based (or centered) educational/learning and application development centers that will advocate and promote our intellectual freedom.

Until this happens, AfRaKa will never be fully liberated. Hence, it is essential to take steps now that will allow the continent to cleanse out the cronies who control oun's educational systems and who serve as nothing more than agents of a new version of Eurasian colonialism.

Currently, we see a rise of many nations that are escaping neo-colonial and religious indoctrination in favor of science and technology. It is important to remember that this will not be an easy task but can be accomplished with serious effort and commitment by local populations and their counsels of leadership. This will allow states to adapt strategies that promote their perspectives as well as their traditional cultures.

In this regard, much of the scholarship and intellectualism of AfRaKaN liberation movements, whether on the continent or elsewhere, have been centered around the theme of achieving complete liberation and, rightfully so but lack a AfRaKaN-centered methodology.

However, this cannot be achieved by education alone because education requires a commitment to funding, of which the modern AfRaKaN state has been deprived of access to financial resources by local and foreign agents.

Furthermore, goods like cocoa and other source/raw products have been exported from the continent at dirt cheap prices while the AfRaKaN imports commercial stage goods like food products, automobiles, computers, diamonds, oil, gas, and other goods that return to AfRaKa with very high tags.

For example, compare the costs of a cocoa bar with that of raw cocoa. As the charts below indicate, the discrepancy is quite disturbing!!

Top Cocoa Producing Countries in the World

Rank	Country	Production (tons)
1	Ivory Coast	1,448,992
2	Ghana	835,466
3	Indonesia	777,500
4	Nigeria	367,000
5	Cameroon	275,000
6	Brazil	256,186
7	Ecuador	128,446
8	Mexico	82,000
9	Peru	71,175
10	Dominican Republic	68,021

FRONTERA
www.frontera.net

Source: UN Food and Agriculture Organization

Africa's Regional Exports Show Ongoing Colonial Legacy

Main export goods of African countries in 2020

Minerals & diamonds
- Gold
- Copper, iron or other ores*
- Diamonds

Energy
- Oil
- Gas

Agriculture, forestry & fishing
- Agricultural products**
- Wood
- Fish

Industry
- Cars
- Boats
- Electrical cables
- Turbines

* other minerals: aluminum, titanium, salt
** cocoa, coffee, tea, nuts, spices, cotton, tobacco, essential oils
Source: The Observatory of Economic Complexity (OED)

statista

Merging IT and Education to obtain a Complete Liberation of AfRaKa would liberate AfRaKa from Imperialism and open new avenues for growth and development. AfRaKa should assert its right to trade with other states directly and not rely on foreign parties to negotiate trade deals on behalf of AfRaKa.

These rights sit at the very foundation of essential freedom, and long as other parties have a financial noose around AFraKa's, the continent will remain a victim of imperialism.

AfRaKaN pedagogy has been reduced into submission as a result of exploitation. In many regards, this has caused a lack of consciousness regarding the identity of AfRaKaN peoples worlidwide.

AfRaKa can no longer remain silent to this obvious threat due to global issues such as climate change.

CHAPTER IV

CHAPTER IV: The Importance of AfRaKaN Investment and the need for Retribution/Reparations

While for many, this may indeed be difficult for those entrenched in a Western perspective and seek to "turn the other cheek," AfRaKa has been the victim of significant crimes against the oldest populations around Geb, and has been reduced to a state of subservience and oppression which the ancient enemies of AfRaKa control. This condition was imposed on the collective representation of AfRaKaN's existence.

The idea presented here is that as "sentient beings," we need to return to our traditional educational values that existed before the invasion during pre-colonial times.

Education can be used as a tool to revert back to perspectives that existed before the periods of imperialism and invasion by the various Caucasian groups, that is to say, the so-called Europeans, his Asiatic cousins, and other cultural and religious groupings such as Muslims, Christians and Hyka Kasu and their break off groupings. The specific focus needs to be placed on the elitist Germanics and their weltanschauung, which inspired rhetoric of the "God" trap as an extension of the Cauc-asian perspective.

Restoring traditional AfRaKaN language, culture, social concepts, and science offers a great deal of promise regarding AfRaKaN development. The advance of technology is primarily connected to an escape from religious indoctrination, which should not be taken lightly.

For this to occur, AfRaKa needs funding either in the form of retributive reparations payments or investment by AfRaKaNs and should avoid development loans. However, due to the international system of imperialism, the AfRaKaN continent has been reduced to a condition of impoverishment that is blocked from loans that do not have strings attached. This to modern enslavement and keeps AfRaKa trapped in an impoverished shackle. In other words, the continent has inherited a financial system that is a leftover remnant of imperialism and which continues to handicap AfRaKaN growth. The AfRaKaN continent has the smell of blood, murder, death, dishonesty, and humiliation all over it, leading to psychological impediments that are difficult and nearly impossible to dismiss. We must remember that this is a reality imposed on the cradle of civilization and not one with indigenous origins.

From an AfRaKan-centered perspective, it is essential that we are able to formalize a concept of an AfRaKaN reality that is fed by technology that allows IT based Data Centers to collect and store information. These centers should be fully developed and maintained by AfRaKaNs and accessible with boundaries such as censorship. Such an approach will encourage investment that should be used to build high-grade technology centers that can focus on educational and development needs, including internal infrastructure improvements for commerce/e-commerce. A primary justification could be the need to improve the flow and management of AfRaKaN currency. Rather in paper, gold, credit, or digital formats, improving financial infrastructure will allow AfRaKaN states to trade internally and Internationally as part fluid and fast past reality.

Such development must be implemented in reasonable terms where they are indeed affordable for AfRaKaN eniyan. Internet access, for example, should be subsidized by the AfRaKAN state as should education and communication in general. This will produce vibrant environments and lead us to amazing new discoveries and possibilities.

Recent studies have shown that affordability impedes the AfRaKAN adaptation of technology.

"In Malawi, people have been paying around 87% of gross national income per capita for 1GB of mobile data. Rwandans only pay 2%. DW examines the reasons for this huge price discrepancy."

To support IT-based development projects, we must first secure the funding needed to finance such objectives by arresting and liberating all the wealth stolen from AfRaKa by the agents and cronies of Caucasian imperialism. Many of these agents continue to live in luxury while their eniyan live in absolute impoverishment. Second, the prices of exports such as oil, gas, gold, diamonds, silicon, and silicon and others should be raised to international levels and not be paid for in paper money with colonial images or faces on them as this reflects colonial interests, but in nuba bars (gold).

A critical step in this regard is first to facilitate the return of AfRaKaNs to AfRaKa and then create channels for intercontinental trade that will allow equivalent values and goods to be exchanged from country to country on equivalent levels. This approach is derived from the foundation of a traditional AfRaKaN system of communalism. It is still more relevant and equitable than the crude materialism characteristic of Western financial systems has been imposed on AfRaKa and Asia by the agents of imperialism and their cronies.

Due to the perception by many that are volatile, AfRaKaN Data Centers should provide the capacity for Web Hosting and design, along with Virtual services and other hosting solutions such as apps. The importance of this is to liberate AFRAKa financially from control and manipulation like a puppet controlled by strings.

Virtual servers could be used to host online social media platforms similar to Youtube, Vimeo, Facebook, and Roku, which are very popular in the AfRaKaN world. If we can pick up a gun, drive a car, or buy a Computer, doesn't that imply that we should be able to produce our own technology independently? In learning to use a computer, you are, in fact partially what it means to build one.

Offering Cloud space will allow AfRaKaN States to host their internet facilities which would not only provide access to the Internet but also to the engines and applications provided by it such as Domain registration and content hosting.

"Economic growth in Sub-Saharan Africa (SSA) is estimated at 4 percent in 2021, up from a contraction in economic activity of 2 percent in 2020. However, growth in the region is expected to decelerate in 2022 amid a global environment with multiple (and new) shocks, high volatility, and uncertainty. The economy is set to expand by 3.6 percent in 2022, down from 4 percent in 2021, as it struggles to pick up momentum amid a slowdown in global economic activity, continued supply constraints, outbreaks of new coronavirus variants, high inflation, and rising financial risks due to high and increasingly vulnerable debt levels."

Implementing local communication facilities, including the Internet, will reduce costs and inspire the development of new tools that could be used to enhance exchange regardless of the format. However, as emphasized earlier, the availability of funding is critical.

"Consider this color-based chart which represents Internet tariffs around the continent. With dark green being the cheapest at less than $1 and red being the most expensive at more than $50

"In Africa, Internet users pay for mobile data more than elsewhere. The disparities in mobile internet tariffs are abysmal, reaching up to more than 1 GB of data."

As indicated below, AfRaKaN connectivity rates are the Highest around Geb. For example, look at Zimbabwe:

"Zimbabwe pays the highest price both in Africa and in the world ($75.20), and countries such as Equatorial Guinea ($65.83) and Saint Helena ($55.47) also pay more than $50. On the contrary, East Africa has the lowest rates, with a gigabyte of mobile data costing ($ 5.93) in Tanzania, ($ 2.91) in Ethiopia, ($ 2.73) in Kenya, (2 $) in Burundi, as well Sudan ($0.68) and the Democratic-Republic of the Congo ($0.88) both pay less than $1 per GB."

"Africa has gotten off on the wrong foot," Amadou Diop, the Senegal-born founder of the digital strategy firm MNS Consulting, says on the topic of digital sovereignty. His company has been hammering out a plan for several months to address the issue, and Diop paints an alarming picture of Africa's shortcomings on the digital front."

To make Internet access more available and valuable in AfRaka, private sector businesses, and local investors should be involved and invited to participate parties. This would include local AfRaKaN investors and international agencies like the AfRaKaN

Development Bank, UNECA, World Bank, IMF, UNDP and others to be heavily involved and provide a means that allows developing nations to reject nepotism and corruption.

Nevertheless, the primary stakeholders and investors should reflect AfRaKaN identities and her perspective(s). As an outcome, this will provide even more of a shield for AfRaKa to protect itself from neo-colonialism and domination by foreign parties. On the technology side, a number of international agencies have attempted to bring affordable Internet to AfRaKa, which usually has strings attached and has been devastating to local economies, as the report below indicates:

"Despite the installation of submarine cables to connect the continent, the price of a gig of mobile internet data remains very high on average."

We should always remember that international funding comes with conditions attached, and AfRaKan states must refuse to be converted into puppets like several states have succumbed to.

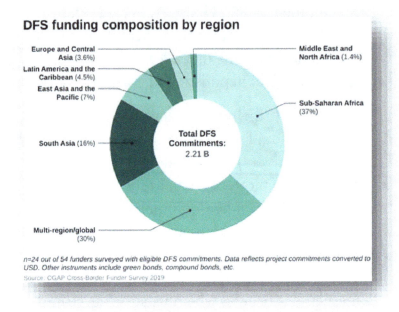

DFS funding composition by region

Europe and Central Asia (3.6%)
Latin America and the Caribbean (4.5%)
East Asia and the Pacific (7%)
Middle East and North Africa (1.4%)
Sub-Saharan Africa (37%)
South Asia (16%)
Multi-region/global (30%)

Total DFS Commitments: 2.21 B

n=24 out of 54 funders surveyed with eligible DFS commitments. Data reflects project commitments converted to USD. Other instruments include green bonds, compound bonds, etc.
Source: CGAP Cross-Border Funder Survey 2019

If not properly regulated and controlled, local entities could face a huge barrier with prostituted puppets leeching off of their own eniyan, including the pseudo-religious groups. This is important because there is a goal of erasing traditional AfRaKaN cultural perspectives from the record of Pr Ankh. AfRaKa must collectively confront this issue right on if the AfRaKaN Identity is to be preserved and protected from the space advocates for which AfRaKa has become a resource breadbasket and, in similar terms or by extension, a pawn of Caucasian imperialism in general.

CHAPTER V

CHAPTER V: Why foreign states should transfer Knowledge, Technology and back to AfRaKa

Reparations would allow AfRaKa to invest heavily in Education, Food production, Medicine, Science, and especially Technology with the goal of being a shining star in the Age of Information and Restoration. And as a result of the expanding use of technology and the appearance of this information age, AfRaKa must assert its sense of identity within consciousness itself. For example, language demonstrates that imperialistic tongues create more harm than benefit for AfraKan eniyan.

Several non-AfRaKaN countries have already begun investing in developing technology in AfRaKa. It seems that Asian nations like China have been very eager to invest in AfRaKaN infrastructure projects. Therefore it is the responsibility of foreign states themselves to reverse their own myopic perspective of AfRaKa and approach trade and other forms of exchange on fair and equivalent terms. For example:

"The presence of Chinese multinational enterprises in Africa brings new technology and knowledge. Yet there is a lack of research on this impact on development in African countries.

Allowing foreign entities to invest in a country's infrastructure can be very dangerous as it could open AfRaKa up to neo-colonial imperialists and their scheme to dominate the flow of resources on a global scale. In this scenario, only the imperialists benefit significantly, leaving AfRaKaN states behind and in greater debt/poverty.

While not as extreme as Western states, China is a perfect example of this paradigm and should adjust its trade relationships with AfRaKa on a more equitable basis. As the article shown below, China built itself up out of extreme impoverishment and may have lessons that AfRaKaNs and other subdued eniyan can learn from:

"China's recent industrial development may be more appropriate for Africa's development than Western models, and the adoption of technological knowledge from Chinese firms may provide a more sustainable path to Africa's development because of cultural, institutional, social, and historical synergies."

This comes with challenges indeed from both sides of the trade relationship and stands as an impediment to honest relations or a situation that is truly beneficial to peace and stability for all here on Geb. AfRaKa does not need connections with parties that have colonial intentions no matter the reason but must partner with those who are interested and, to some extent, dedicated to furthering what can be labeled "global balance," "harmony," or development.

To this extent, we must thoroughly investigate the intentions of those seeking to invest in AfRaKa, as the continent has been plagued by imperialists who only sought to strip the continent of her resources. For example, like the West, China must be willing to invest in AfRaKa while not being involved in AfRaKaN political and social/cultural affairs. This should not be an issue since China depends on goods and food supplies produced in AfRaKa. However, China just let the West should inherit the perspective of inherent right and should pay equitable prices for AfRaKa goods.

As the following quotation indicates, China experienced similar historical conditions and manage to institute development policies to raise itself to the age of information.

"However, major barriers may exist to transferring appropriate technology and knowledge. Findings from our study in the construction industry in Ghana suggest an absence of specific technology and knowledge transfer policies and strategies, with human resource development practices, language, and some cultural issues also creating barriers. Bidding practices of Chinese firms investigated also appear to militate against successful technology and knowledge transfers to local partners and staff. Yet there appears to be unrealized potential that has not been addressed by firms. We suggest measures that may be taken to realize this potential and point to implications for policy and future research on the development potential of China in Africa.:."

Like many parts of Asia, the lack of technological develop and infrastructure kidnapped AfRaKa, which is an issue that needs to be addressed. Technology can lead to numerous possibilities that could be very beneficial for the continent in terms of development. Not only will this spark growth, but it will also lead to more equalitarian societies as eniyan moves forward to embrace their traditional heritage. And as a result, a union of culture and technology has the potential to create new roads of possibility that can be free of stigma and dogma and liberate the AfRaKan worlid from the ills of imperialism and ignorance.

In this sense, education, medicine, and health care become even more valuable and vital to AfRAKAN development schemes. Digital apps could be designed and produced at a very lost cost and become effective means to disseminate information and knowledge and scientific literacy.

I have personally benefitted from the miracles of modern medicine and science as my recovery from life-threatening health issues was facilitated by a combination of both. Currently, my health is being monitored and controlled by medical devices like apps, a defibrillator, a glucose meter, and smartwatch that I use on a daily basis. While recovering, I began to think of how AfRaKaNs are transitioning needlessly due to issues caused by poor health and the inability to afford adequate health care. If anything in this country should be socialized it's Medicine and Health Care. I also realized that much of what I had gathered to restore my health was from either online resources or thru apps. Amazon and other digital tools provide a great service that can be used when looking for alternative sources of information.

The condition of my disability served as the primary foundation as well as the impetus behind my path of restoration to good health and stability. My limited IT skills helped me recover elements of my skills but only partially. This led me to conclude that in this age of Information, we should use modern technology to improve the condition of eniyan in general, which is a process that can be accomplished by studying traditional languages, medicine, science, and other educational sources. From here we can develop AfRaKan tools based on AfRaKan needs and not profit. This would include IT tools like database repositories, apps, websites, and others, incorporating modern scientific principles and methodology.

We need to understand just how critical this is because an

AfRaKaN's perspective actually defines our identity and is a crucial element in the progression of our psychological health.

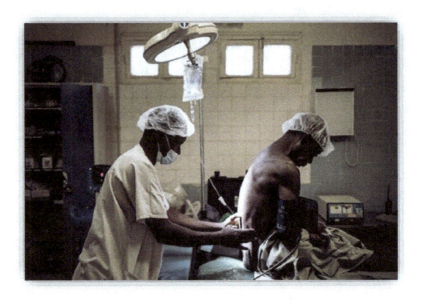

Medicine provides a gateway standard that should be used to measure the level of progress in an Information driven reality.

This would enable us to evaluate the efficiency of governing institutions as well as the quality of leadership within our societies.

CHAPTER VI

CHAPTER VI: The need in AfRAKA for more Technology and Research Centers

To empower AfRaKaNs to achieve such goals, we should focus our attention and resources on infrastructure development and the construction of Research Centers in this regard. We will evaluate this more in the next chapter by reviewing the achievements made over the past 30 orbits. We will evaluate existing strategies to determine how efficient they are and point out opportunities for improvement.

However, let's continue with articulating the justification of Data Centers and the possible benefits that can be derived from them. AfRaKaNs should own Data Centers that can be placed in local and international locations and place storage and communication devices in spaces that reflect traditional AfRaKaN concepts, culture, and values.

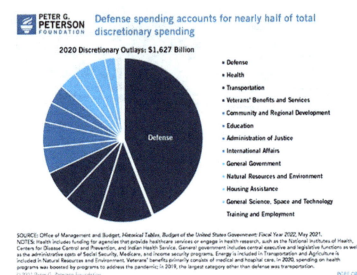

PETER G. PETERSON FOUNDATION

Defense spending accounts for nearly half of total discretionary spending

2020 Discretionary Outlays: $1,627 Billion

- Defense
- Health
- Transportation
- Veterans' Benefits and Services
- Community and Regional Development
- Education
- Administration of Justice
- International Affairs
- General Government
- Natural Resources and Environment
- Housing Assistance
- General Science, Space and Technology
- Training and Employment

SOURCE: Office of Management and Budget, Historical Tables, Budget of the United States Government: Fiscal Year 2022, May 2021.
NOTES: Health includes funding for agencies that provide healthcare services or engage in health research, such as the National Institutes of Health, Centers for Disease Control and Prevention, and Indian Health Service. General government includes central executive and legislative functions as well as the administrative costs of Social Security, Medicare, and income security programs. Energy is included in Transportation and Agriculture is included in Natural Resources and Environment. Veterans' benefits primarily consists of medical and hospital care. In 2020, spending on health programs was boosted by programs to address the pandemic; in 2019, the largest category other than defense was transportation.
© 2021 Peter G. Peterson Foundation

PGPF.ORG

While many imperialist states use data centers to store information, it collects from populations around the worlid, which is often used for espionage and allows imperial (industrial) states to engage in advanced levels of research in the areas of space exploration, weapon production, and medicine. This serves as a wall of protection that now dominate the worlid. For example, as the chart below indicates, these two segments consume the largest percentage of the US budget.

Here's the same budget of USSR:

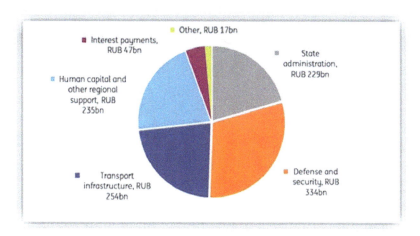

And this is a chart that shows how China increased its funding for defense budget by 7.1% in 2022

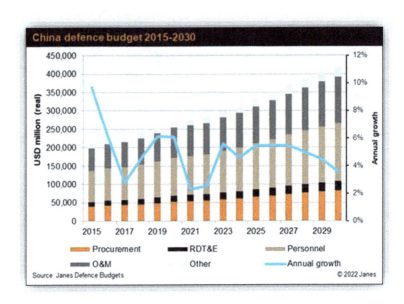

Here's another graph of space countries with the largest budgets:

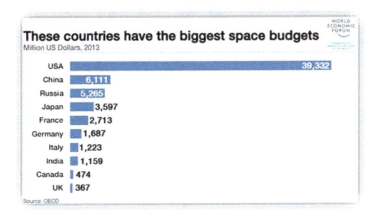

WORLD ECONOMIC FORUM

These countries have the biggest space budgets
Million US Dollars, 2013

USA	39,332
China	6,111
Russia	5,265
Japan	3,597
France	2,713
Germany	1,687
Italy	1,223
India	1,159
Canada	474
UK	367

Source: OECD

In many regards, it becomes evident that the construction of the modern state is being driven by a goal of supporting the international space program. We have experienced a migration from feudalism to capitalism as well as from socialism and communism.

These systems accentuate a very materialistic expression of existence that are non-Communal and in conflict with Netcher regarding the traditional formation of the state and the infrastructure associated with it. Marxism, for example, is the closest concept Europeans have in comparison with communalism. However, it continues to remain handicapped by its allegiance to the crude materialism that's present in the Caucasian worlidview.

The underlying component that is the key to them all is using existence as a resource generator to finance Space exploration. All the financial powers mentioned earlier have thriving Space programs that, in addition to being funded, require defense. Therefore, existence is paying a price that supports the agenda of a small grouping of Elitists who dominate this reality and have planned an escape.

This explains why Climate change has a huge influence on technological development. But for the poor masses, issues associated with health, food, and the quality of life are more essential questions requiring great attention. At the same time, there is enough wealth and resources to facilitate them both, which suggests that only the greed of the elite few is responsible for the current environment of poverty and hatred that we find almost entirely around Geb. Eliminating this class would allow the creation of a more netcheral world. And in my opinion, technological development is a great tool that can be very useful in terms of achieving development goals.

CHAPTER VII

CHAPTER VII: Using Information Technology to combat the hegemony in international trade relations.

As a Systems Engineer and IT specialist, I was often able to ship PCs we made here in the US back to various countries in AfRaKa. What amazed me the most was that the PCs we would assemble and sell in the States for an average of between $900 and $1500 would sell for $2500 to$3000 in many parts of AfRaKa. Of course tariffs and shipping cost increased the costs significantly but the price gap allowed to understand just how difficult it was to access IT and the lack of local capacity to build them at cheaper rates. Now some of this was due AfRaKaN crooks and pimps who leeched off of their communities, but when looked at the whole setup, you quickly see how it benefitted the materialism of Caucasians.

However, as an employee of The Leland Initiative, USAID, and UNECA, I was heavily involved in transferring technology to AfRaKa. I assisted 52 of 54 countries to connect with the Internet and provided Web development training to many communities. Additionally, I would travel around the continent extensively and set up cyber cafes for business owners, ship computers, and assist educational centers in their connectivity needs. These activities were financed by the international organizations I mentioned earlier. I realized later in my career that while international donors paid for these financial costs, AfRaKa would pay in terms of her cultural independence and political freedom.

While I was able to accomplish much of the same here in the US, my experience promoting IT always provided me with a sense of intellectual pride and an element of peace and tranquility knowing that I could do even more in the land of Iya (AfRaKa).

During that time, many were unaware of computers and the functionality IT had to offer, so the Leland Initiative and the UNECA allowed the team I was affiliated with become ambassadors of ICTs for development, which was received with a lot of gratitude and appreciation.

Geb doesn't need to be dominated by a few elitists whose errant policies have reduced the quality of existence that keeps Geb in constant conflict. We have been converted into pawns and agents of this self-destructive process as opposed to being agents of modernity,

Unfortunately, many oppressed and subjugated worlid continue to be subjects and servants of the international system of Caucasian imperialism, which parades itself as modernization. Furthermore, as a result of this perspective, many in the developing worlid are now find themselves dependent on or addicted to Caucasian sources and rely on this relationship to provide the basic necessities of modern existence. When we need food, medicine, a car, medicine, or education, almost all of these resources are imported from foreign and Caucasian-owned states at very high tarrif.

On the other hand, resources and goods that are exported from AfRaKa are usually valued as being very cheap. This by itself conditions trade relations and favors the Eurasian seller, not the AfRaKaN buyer. It also favors the Eurasian

buyer over the AfRaKan seller on financial terms equating to modern enslavement. This implies that an open or free society doesn't exist and is actually nothing more than a slogan used to protect and promote Caucasian hegemony and dominance within financial sectors globally.

In contrast, the culture of submission must be rejected by a powerful renewal of access to information by the oppressed. To protect and promote the Eurocentric perspective, the English language is a covert attempt to convert populations worlidwide into Germanics.

CHAPTER VIII

CHAPTER VIII: Is antagonism the primary catalyst behind the AfRaKaN Information Age?

The quick answer is no! Optimism is an empowering force , so it should be stated that AfRaKaN advances are motivated primarily by scientific discovery and technological development, which AfRaKa needs to embraced with a serious level of commitment. In fact, the AfRaKaN world (Geb)is embracing technology even more as it attempts to escape the shackles of imperialism. However, as AfRaKa continues to embrace technology, it must adopt an AfRaKaN and comprised of a compilation of cultural perspectives and driven by necessity and not greed.

In this regard, technology must be accompanied by education with the primary focus being on science and technical training. This is because before dismissing concepts, we must evaluate current efforts to measure their value and discern whether they provide value for the AfRaKaN reality and can be helpful in terms of our development or not. While our perepective should remain positive in orientation we also not dismissive the regressive or negative energy as well. In battle a segun segun must be consciously aware of both and rely on them whenever required and by any means necessary!!! At the same time we must recognize the potential IT and the Information Age has at large. Currently AfRaKa's borders are wide open and vulnerable due to the domininace of caucasion perceptions and his control of recourses around the world and his of IT to shield his objectives.

Our analysis also serves as a justification for creating a new paradigm, as my awon ebi over at Same Tree Different Branch Publishing have outlined within the concept or perspective of Kimoyo. On the other hand, we must reject the rhetoric we encounter from all the charlatans and financial pimps from the pseudo camps we experience as AfRaKaN eniyan. Our development needs require us to be focused more on science than with the indoctrination and religious spookism which has been imposed on us by the Asiatics. Otherwise, the consequence is that we become promoters of imperialists which continues to cause us to promote a unified anti-indigenous perspective which could be used as we continue advocate for a renewal of AfRaKaN development.

This is in complete opposition to what the elitist HK class has done, which is to use an Asiatic systems of mind control to usurp the physical and creative energies of the masses for the purpose of financing their interests while the poor masses pay the bill for their escape route to another planet. A large portion of these resources is being used to finance the space program with complete disregard for the interests of the impoverished eniyan.

So just like the Hem Neter Roger Rodney taught in How Europe Underdeveloped AfRaKaN impoverished states continue to be a basket of resources for Cauc-asian imperialism, which now carries the name of Space Exploration. Instead of telling the scientific truth about the threat of climate change, using mind control techniques and IT in general, the cauc-asian seems to prefer using such immoral techniques as subjugation, enslavement and cultural annihilation to finance their own self-centered escape.

However, as AfRaKaNs, we must reject all forms of any kind of imperialism so that we can build a new rendition of our traditional AfRaKaN perspective. The challenge here is dealing with the chocolate-chipped oreos who pretend to be AfRaKaN but instead are pawns, agents of their Asiatic "Father." To this extent, you'll find it much harder to fight against the chocolate chipper than you will the vanilla wafer regarding a true AfRaKaN perspective and the communities it is design to represent.

In many ways, this shows the importance of an intellectual form of resistance that stems from eliminating and rejecting the intellectual and mental control techniques deployed by the global Elitists who control the entire "world". This will be a tough obstacle for the impoverished to overcome due to the level of technique which has elevated exploitation to perfection.

To combat this expanding trend, priority and focus must be dedicated to a re-discovery of traditional AfRaKan language, culture, concepts of existence that are built firmly on the principles of Science and Technology. Some of us may have read The Mis-Education of the AfRaKaN (NEgrowth) by Carter G. Goodson which discusses this in detail. The issue the AfRaKaNs has is that for every successful attempt we accomplish in moving AfRaKa forward are enemies usurp that energy from it and advances two steps ahead of us using technology. We mistakenly conclude that we are contributing to the well being of this society at large but instead have dug deeper holes for ourselves. And this is because we have become addicted to trying to fit-in opposed to liberating our eniyan from the shackles of enslavement.

Like Franz Fanon taught us we are AfRaKaN in khet (skin/body) but Caucasian intellectually!!! But this is due to our lack of investment in technology and our willing to submit to our own subjugation.

Our inability to study our condition meticulously has left us behind in terms of technological advancement. Instead of focusing on stone age forms of indoctrination we should be more focused on scientific methodology, i.e., exploration and experimentation. Knowledge is Superior to "beweef"!!

What technical education does is lift us out of the realm of ignorance imposed on the Worlid by Asiatic (centered) imperialists and add us to problem that poisoning Geb.

CHAPTER IX

CHAPTER IX: Solar-Powered and Efficient Transportation in the battle against Climate Change

Climate change is presenting some huge challenges to this reality. More studies indicate that existence is under serious threat and could be eliminated within a short time. To address this threat, a number of measures have either been taken or are in development that has the potential to combat global warming. This includes a transfer to electric vehicles, switching towards eating more health-oriented food, such as vegetarian and Vegan diets, and switching to biodegradable products to reduce the production of waste and garbage.

An issue here is that the current cost of food supplies and climate change has a measurable impact on food supplies. According to a recent report by the International Monetary Fund

"Food supplies and prices are especially vulnerable to climate change in sub-Saharan Africa because of a lack of resilience to climatic" IMF."

Since the goal here has been dominated by profit, fragile farmers do not have the resources or means to protect their crops from the multi-national corps (Big Farm); they become victims of GMO farming schemes that contaminate local farming techniques and eat up the soil and make it more difficult to healthy food supplies.

At the time, the cost of food increased significantly, making it far more difficult for the poor.

"Staple food prices in sub-Saharan Africa surged by an average of 23.9 percent in 2020-22—the most since the 2008 global financial crisis. This is commensurate to an 8.5 percent rise in the cost of a typical food consumption basket (beyond generalized price increases)."

Imagine a world in which climate change, food scarcity, and poverty as insignificant because there is no food to sell or eat. Starvation is so steep that nothing can be done but sit, watch, and suffer. International events are leading to the possibility that one of the catalysts for the escalation of the devastating possibilities could be a nuclear confrontation. I wouldn't see either, but we do have a class among us who have become so desperate that they could trigger such an event.

While the possibility of such an event may seem vague now, given the geopolitical state of Geb, we seem to not be able to understand how this impacts markets. In other words, as food availability becomes scarce, the prices of food become more and more expensive, and what the Eurasian systems have seemed to be suggesting is that if you don't/can't "work," you will not be paid and if you are not able to pay then you are not allowed to eat. This means that you primarily become a victim of imperialism and might as well transition, especially if you support religion or faith. It seems contradictory, but the cauc-asian state's whole design is nothing more than a pipe dream. If we take into consideration, we see that global economic and political trends allow us to look deeper into the current crisis and a further analysis that will enable us to detect just how the Cauc-asian powers are using food scarcity and other basic necessities of existence to force communities worldwide into submission. The quote below provides some good insights in this regard:

"The relative strength of a country's currency is another driver as it affects the costs of imported food items. We find that a 1 percent depreciation in real effective exchange rates increases the price of highly imported staples by an average of 0.3 percent."

I am afraid that all of the energy being organized to deal with food shortage is actually falling dead ears and eyes. Awon eniyan doesn't seem to care, nor does it question the rising prices or foot shortages in the market. Instead, attention is directed at pseudo-intellectualism, a descendent of the Germanic (HK)"Black" trap.

AfRaKaN development is crippled by its limitation to non-scientific perspectives that are deeply infused with culture and language which provides the AfRaKaN with tools needed to restore its own perspective of existence.

https://www.imf.org/en/Blogs/Articles/2022/09/26/africa-food-prices-are-soaring-amid-high-import-reliance

However, climate change is not the only problem farmers face and can be a victim of exaggeration in terms of analysis. Weather trends seem to suggest that it provides a sound justification for investing in knowledge and technology as a remedy.

"Climate change has not been the root cause of the continent's regional famines. Decade after decade, hunger crises have stemmed from a familiar set of circumstances: poor agricultural conditions—including adverse weather, insect infestations, drought, or improper land use—mixed with geopolitical instability. But climate change isn't entirely blameless, either. Like an earthquake that just won't stop, climate change breaks foundations that are already weak and also makes it harder to repair and refortify while the ground is continually shaking." IMF

A serious question here is if climate change is an effect, what is the cause? While a portion of this can be blamed on Necher, that doesn't account for the greater portion caused by eniyan.

In my opinion, this is a direct affect of Industrialization that limits the capacity of eniyan to not only deal with climate change but the development needs of modernity. Insect infestation can also present a large threat to depleted food industry, making the pain, famine, and other crises even worse. In the ancient Tanehesi/Demet/Nubian/Cush portion of AfRaKa:

"The current swarms of locusts are the most serious outbreak in decades, affecting Somalia, Ethiopia, Kenya, Eritrea, and most recently, Tanzania and Uganda. The locusts could fly into South Sudan, a country whose population is already struggling with high levels of hunger. The swarms are huge, in North-Eastern Kenya, one swarm was measured to be 37 miles long and 25 miles wide."

This suggests that insect infections can cause just as much destructive damage as climate charge or drought. It must be noted that AfRaKaN is not a safe haven against global crises but serves as the safest location to shield AfRaKANs from too much exposure from existential imperialism.

 Yet, because so many of us are caught in a spelled cast reality, we can't see; we refuse to see what's going on and actually contribute to the problem. Instead of existing in a perpetual state of ignorance and submission, we must take a unified stance to demand our awon ebi and our dignity. In addition to this, traditional AfRaKaN was highly based on farming. Still, like other segments of the economy, much of this capacity has been controlled or wiped out by Eurasians and mega-farms. AfRaKa has become the breadbasket of both the Cauc and the Asiatics.

"Around 45% of food supply in South Africa is wasted, impacting the economy, water security and contributing to climate change, according to research."

CHAPTER X

CHAPTER X: A Brief Look at AfRaKaN
Initiatives to Explore Space

I am convinced that the underlining that is driving the AfRaKaN interests in spsce exploration can actually be placed in two camps. One is based on a sense of understanding the discoveries of modern science. The other is understanding the changing times and the need to rid the planet of the so-called "White" elicits.

I think a third option is also available, and that's where you don't choose either side and decide the method is questionable. The objective of colonizing another planet is the best option if existence will continue to be present on this planet.

Therefore, from this perspective, space exploration has merit, but since most of, while not have the means to go or no intention of leaving Geb like me, I think the Cauc-Asian should subsidize the construction of his great escape route with his own resources his or when he needs them from others.

I've been doing a lot of research since I purchased a new telescope and have learned that AfRaKaNs are active participants in this rapidly advancing branch of science; for example, many AfRaKaN countries have launched satellites into space and have established space programs. According to The Economist:

"The small cube—Nigeria's first satellite and only the second launched by a sub-Saharan African country—did not just watch a storm, it provoked one, too. British politicians and a taxpayers' pressure group called for a halt in development aid, saying Nigeria did not need help if it could afford a space program. Still, the sums spent on space by African countries back then were tiny. South Africa's SUNSAT, the region's first satellite, was built by students at Stellenbosch University and hitched a free ride on a NASA rocket. Nigeria's spacecraft cost just $13m."

As the article below demonstrates, how Nigeria's persistence has allowed the state to push forward with the creation of a space agency and demonstrates that the Caucasian states will not have a monopoly control over space exploration and that it is better to engage in multiple perspectives when it comes to the potential to discover another location where existence might and could be possible.

Due to the potential of climate change to produce an extinction event, it is good that AfRaKaN states are getting involved in this emerging area of science. Because in order to avoid what could be an extinction-level event, the international community has to step up to the table and demonstrate a solid commitment to space exploration and AfRaKaN participation on multiple levels. AfRaKaN material resources are not the only area where AfRaKan contrition would be beneficial. AfRaKaN perspectives offer a different approach to scientific exploration as it incorporates concepts of balance and harmony which will be extremely valuable during long space voyages.

The best way that AfRaKa can add value to space exploration is to provide training and assistance to allow space pioneers to overcome the limitations of their addiction to crude materialism. Dealing with the threat of climate change as a unified team would help increase the possibility of success in space missions.

Jun 17th, 2021

We've seen several cases where we failed to take a unified stance voluntarily to promote and project a collective sense of collective commonality. The American experience has provided us with several perfect examples, like the response to Hurricane Katrina. The support from AfRaKa is not well known by many, and we choose instead to tear AfRaKa down. Yet, we do have a record of AfRaKaN involvement in supporting relief efforts. This demonstrates the ability of AfRaKaN states to provide strong and adequate levels of technical support in terms of scientific research. Consider the quote below for example:

"IN THE HOURS after Hurricane Katrina slammed into America in 2005, destroying large parts of New Orleans, the people coordinating the disaster response urgently needed satellite pictures to show them what they were facing. The first images were not from the constellations launched by NASA or the space agencies of other rich countries. They were beamed to Earth by a small Nigerian spacecraft launched from Russia just two years earlier." (5)

With climate change becoming a global threat and with mostly Cauc-Asians being affected, I think many eniyan are skeptical and hesitant. So, the question becomes why should non-cauc-asians actually care, and what keeps Africans and others from reciprocating with a similar expression of anger and hostility that many of us have experienced throughout modern history?

We have limited options to being usurped into a wide-ranging initiative to conquer the Geb with mental indoctrination of eniyan. In this regard, moving forward with AfRaKaN expressions of technological advancement is the best option, given the existential condition of the continent where resources have been depleted, and poverty rates are high.

The threat and impact of global warming suggest that investment in space exploration is a necessity and not an option. Maybe this will explain why Nigeria has also invested heavily in space exploration while dealing with the potential financial instability. For example:

"The small cube—Nigeria's first satellite and only the second launched by a sub-Saharan African country—did not just watch a storm; it provoked one, too. British politicians and a taxpayers' pressure group called for a halt in development aid, saying Nigeria did not need help if it could afford a space program. Still, the sums being spent on space by African countries back then were tiny. South Africa's SUNSAT, the region's first satellite, was built by students at Stellenbosch University and hitched a free ride on a NASA rocket. Nigeria's spacecraft cost just $13m. "(6)

I suspect that the level of investment has increased due to recent weather trends and rising costs. Yet AfRaKaN space programs are popping up in several locations around the continent.

"In the past few years, however, the continent has dashed into space. The most recent orbital enthusiast is Mauritius, which put up a satellite on June 3rd. At least 20 African countries now have space programs. These include heavyweights like Egypt, Algeria, and Nigeria and smaller countries like Ghana. In 2019 another five African countries launched satellites, bringing Africa's total in orbit that year to 41." (7)

It seems that we will have to put our historical grievances aside momentarily to prevent the possible extinction of existence here on Geb.

CHAPTER XI

CHAPTER XI: CONCLUSION

AfRaKa should become more adamant about the Retribution owed by Colonial Powers as well as the protection of all her resources from exploitation. Instead, the continent is in a ripe position to educate its youth so that they can become more involved and active in science and technological development.

However, to accomplish this objective, the imperialist states must also return AfRaKa's stolen eniyan and her Nuba Bars.

Simultaneously, young AfRaKaNs must stand up and challenge the cultural perspectives imposed on AfRaKaN and restore the traditional views of those who walked before us.

The continent has much to look forward to as the influence of imperialism continues to decay, and this opens new paths for development. As a cornerstone, technology should be fully embraced. This masked a focus on ICT and App development as a valuable tool for restoring the traditional AfRaKaN perspective regarding existence. In closing, we should never forget that......... Tomorrow...........is

not a given..........but yesterday
was.........and today..........is still..........in
the process of being given!!!

Bibliography

Quotations

(1).https://www.imf.org/en/Blogs/Articles/2022/09/14/how-africa-can-escape-chronic-food-insecurity-amid-climate-change

(2).https://www.cips.org/supply-management/news/2021/august/almost-half-of-south-africa-food-supply-is-wasted-says-study/

(3).https://www.imf.org/en/Blogs/Articles/2022/09/26/africa-food-prices-are-soaring-amid-high-import-reliance

(4).https://www.nytimes.com/2005/08/30/us/hurricane-katrina-slams-into-gulf-coast-dozens-are-dead.html

(5). The Economist:
https://www.economist.com/middle-east-and-

africa/2021/06/17/africa-is-blasting-its-way-
into-the-space-race

(6). The Economist:
https://www.economist.com/middle-east-and-
africa/2021/06/17/africa-is-blasting-its-way-
into-the-space-race

 (7). https://time.com/5784323/un-locust-east-
africa/

(8). https://time.com/6220057/climate-change-
africa-food-crisis/

Books

Llaila Melanin What Makes Black People
Black! New York: Seaburn Publishing Group,
2009

AfRaKan Academy of Sciences. Workshop on
Science and Technology Communication
Networks in AfRaKa. Nairobi: AfRaKan
Academy of Science, 1993

Balaam, David N., and Michael Veseth, eds.
Introduction to International Political Econo
New Jersey: Prentice Hall, 1996

Baradat, Leon P. Political Ideologies. New
Jersey: Prentice Hall, 1994

Billet, Bret L. Investment behavior of
Multinational Corporations in Developing
Areas. New Brunswick: Transaction Publishers,
1991

Clough, Michael. Free at Last?. New York:
Council on Foreign Relations Press, 1992

Dalley, Stephanie. Myths from Mesopotamia.
New York: Oxford Univeristy Press, 1992

Drew, Eileen P., and F. Gordon Foster, eds.
Information Technology in Selected Countries.
Tokyo: United Nations University, 1994

Dubois, W.E.B. The World and AfRaKa. New
York: International Publishers, 1965

Fieldhouse, D.K.. Black AfRaKa: 1940 1980.
Boston: Unwin Hyman, 1986

Haggard, Stephan, and Robert R. Kaufman,
eds. The Politics of Economic Adjustment.
Princeton: Princeton University Press, 1992

Harbeson, John W., and Donald Rothchild, eds.
Afiica in World Politics. Boulder: Westview
Press, 1991

Leedy, Paul D. Practical Research: Planning and Design . 5th ed. New York: Macmillan Publishing Company, 1993

Men-Ib Iry-Maat, Wudjau. A Beginner's

Introduction to Medew Netcher

2nd ed. USA Wudjau Men-Ib Iry-Maat, 2016

Moran, Theodore H. Multinational Corporations. Massachusetts: Lexington Books, 1985

National Research Council, Office of International Affairs, Bridge Builders. Washington: National Academy Press, 1996

Obenga, Theophile. African Philosophy. USA: Brawtley Press, 2015

Piesie, Kofi. Beautiful Lessons About Kimoyo USA: Same Tree Different Branch Publishing, 2021

Piesie, Kofi. Spear Masters, USA: Kofi. Piesie
Research Team, 2021

Rodney,Walter. How Europe Underdeveloped
AfRaKa. Washington: Howard University
Press, 1974

Reid, Garfield. Misconceptions &
Misinformation by the Black Hebrew Israelites
Vol 1. USA: Garfield Reid, 2021

Rosenbloom, Richard. Technology and
Information Transfer. Boston: Harvard
University Press, 1970

Sandbrook, Richard. The Politics of AfRaKa's
Economic Recovery. New York: Cambridge

University Press, 1993

Segal, Ronald. Islam's Black Slaves. New
York: Farrar, Straus and Giroux, 2002

Shibre, Zewdie, and Abdulhamid Bedri, eds. Regional Development Problems in AfRaKa . Addis

Ababa: Institute of Development Research, 1993

Slater, Robert O., Barry M. Schutz, and Steven R. Dorr, eds., Global Transformation and the

Third World. Boulder: Lynne Rienner Publishers, 1992

Steindorff, George and Seele, Keith C. When Egypt Ruled the East. Chicago: The University of Chicago Press, 1942

Turabian, Kate. A Manual for Writers. 5th ed. Chicago: University of Chicago, 1987

Weiss, Thomas G., and Merl A. Kessler, eds. Third World Security in the Post Cold War Era

Boulder: Lynne Reinner Publishers, 1991

Weston, Alan F. Information Technology in a Democra . Cambridge: Harvard University Press, 1971

Articles, Papers and Public Documents

da Costa, Peter. "AfRaKa Communication: Internet   A Statist Model", Addis Ababa:

International Press Service, 10 September 1996,

National Telecommunications and Information Administration, "U.S. Goals and Objectives for the

Information Society and Development Conference", prepared remarks of Vice President Al Gore, delivered via satellite to the Information Society and Development Conference in Midrand, South AfRaKa(May 13, 1996)

Semret, Nemo. "Unleashing AfRaKa's Potential: The Technological Reasons for Open and

Competitive Cybercommunications", a paper
delivered at The Second Annual Meeting of the
AfRaKa Scientific Society, Washington, June
22, 1996

Burka, Lauren P. "A Hypertext History of
Multi-User Dimensions." MUD History. 1993.
http://www.utopia.com/talent/lpb/muddex/essay
(2 Aug. 1996).

Fine Arts." Dictionary of Cultural Literacy. 2nd
ed. Ed. E. D. Hirsch, Jr., Joseph F. Kett, and
James Trefil. Boston: Houghton Mifflin. 1993.
INSO Corp. America Online. Reference
Desk/Dictionaries/Dictionary of Cultural
Literacy (20 May 1996)

AfRaKan Academy of Sciences. Workshop on
Science and Technology Communication
Networks in AfRaKa. Nairobi: AfRaKan
Academy of Science, 1993

Balaam, David N., and Michael Veseth, eds.
Introduction to International Political Econo
New Jersey: Prentice Hall, 1996

Baradat, Leon P. Political Ideologies. New Jersey: Prentice Hall, 1994

Billet, Bret L. Investment behavior of Multinational Corporations in Developing Areas. New Brunswick: Transaction Publishers, 1991

Clough, Michael. Free at Last? New York: Council on Foreign Relations Press, 1992

Dalley, Stephanie. Myths from Mesopotamia. New York: Oxford University Press, 1992

Drew, Eileen P., and F. Gordon Foster, eds. Information Technology in Selected Countries. Tokyo: United Nations University, 1994

Dubois, W.E.B. The World and AfRaKa. New York: International Publishers, 1965

Fieldhouse, D.K.. Black AfRaKa: 1940 1980.
Boston: Unwin Hyman, 1986

Haggard, Stephan, and Robert R. Kaufman,
eds. The Politics of Economic Adjustment.
Princeton: Princeton University Press, 1992

Harbeson, John W., and Donald Rothchild, eds.
Afiica in World Politics. Boulder: Westview
Press, 1991

Leedy, Paul D. Practical Research: Planning
and Design . 5th ed. New York: Macmillan
Publishing Company, 1993

Men-Ib Iry-Maat, Wudjau. A Beginner's

Introduction to Medew Netcher

2nd ed. USA Wudjau Men-Ib Iry-Maat, 2016

Moran, Theodore H. Multinational
Corporations. Massachusetts: Lexington Books,
1985